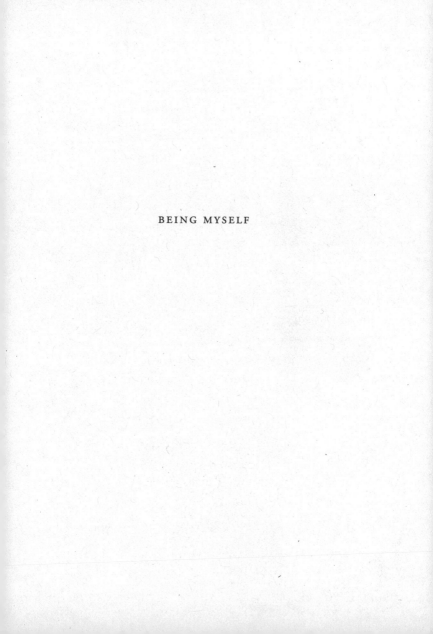

BEING MYSELF

THE ESSENCE OF MEDITATION SERIES

BEING MYSELF

Rupert Spira

SAHAJA

newharbinger
publications

SAHAJA PUBLICATIONS

PO Box 887, Oxford OX1 9PR
www.sahajapublications.com

A co-publication with New Harbinger Publications
5674 Shattuck Ave.
Oakland, CA 94609
United States of America

Distributed in Canada by Raincoast Books

Designed by Rob Bowden

Printed in Canada

ISBN 978-1-68403-162-7

Library of Congress Cataloging-in-Publication Data on file with publisher

In Thy light shall we see light

PSALM 36:9

CONTENTS

Foreword ix
Acknowledgements xv
Note to the Reader xvii

CHAPTER 1
The Sense of Being Myself 1

CHAPTER 2
Our Naked Being 11

CHAPTER 3
I Am 23

CHAPTER 4
Our Self Is the Knowing Element in All Experience 35

CHAPTER 5
The Nature of Our Self 43

CHAPTER 6
The Memory of Our Eternity 51

CHAPTER 7
The Unveiling of Myself 63

CHAPTER 8
The Joy of Being 73

CHAPTER 9
The World and Myself Are One 83

CHAPTER 10
Peace and Happiness Lie in the Depths of Our Being 89

CHAPTER 11
Establishment in Our True Nature 97

CHAPTER 12
Keep the Name 'I' Sacred 105

CHAPTER 13
The Divine Name 113

There is a common discernment that runs like a thread through the world's spiritual and philosophic traditions. It has been gestured to by many names in many languages, but the name by which it is best known is the perennial philosophy.

Although its lineaments may be traced through comparative study of the world's scriptures, mystics and sages, its essential tenets may be derived from first principles. One begins with the metaphysical Absolute, that Ultimate Reality or Supreme Principle indicated by such terms as the Godhead of Meister Eckhart, the Good of Plato, the One of Plotinus, Ibn al-'Arabi's Divine Essence, Shankaracharya's attributeless supreme Reality, the eternal Tao of Lao Tzu and the primordial Ground of Dzogchen.

The Absolute is necessarily without limitation, restriction or determination. It is at once unique and an all-encompassing totality. It is, of necessity, partless, as the finite and relative could have no common measure with Its absoluteness and infinitude. Manifestation arises in consequence of Its infinitude or universal possibility, yet manifestation is neither separate from nor identical to the Absolute.

Ultimately, there are not two realities, the Absolute and manifestation; rather, the Absolute alone is real and yet manifestation is ultimately not other than the Absolute. The human being, as part of manifestation, participates in the inherently paradoxical relation between manifestation and the Absolute. Just as manifestation is not other than the Absolute, so we also share this indivision.

The Spirit or Self is at once the immanent presence of the Absolute and the true ground of our subjectivity. It is our very principle and essence, through which we derive our entire existence. The realisation of our identity with the Spirit or Self is at once our perfection, our liberation and our return to the Absolute, from which we have never in fact been apart. This realisation stands at once as the fulfilment and the confirmation of the perennial philosophy.

Yet how may this unitive identity be realised? Each tradition, with its attendant path, provides its own means, but such teaching and spiritual practice may only lead to the realisation's outer boundary. There is a chasm yet to be leapt. In Plato's *Seventh Letter*, he speaks of the sudden passage from discursive reasoning to intellective vision. As with the seeress Diotima's description in Plato's *Symposium* of the apprehension of the Form of the Beautiful, the vision comes 'of a sudden', revealed to the soul as a spontaneous, immediate presence:

> For a thing of this kind cannot be expressed by words like other disciplines, but by long familiarity, and living in the conjunction with the thing itself, a light as it were leaping from a fire will on a sudden be enkindled in the soul, and there itself nourish itself. *

In a similar manner, the course of instruction in Advaita Vedanta is presented in terms of a threefold process of deepening engagement: hearing the teaching, reflecting upon it and stabilising oneself in it. It is through this process of engagement – at once rational and experiential – that direct insight or realisation may arise. The 'moment' of how this may come about is a mystery, but the process is not: it is the result of skilful teaching suitably received.

* Translated by Thomas Taylor.

Rupert Spira is precisely such a skilled teacher, one who speaks at once out of a depth of realised understanding and a breadth of practical experience in guiding seekers towards this fundamental insight. An ancient spiritual metaphor contrasts green wood with dry wood as a measure of the readiness of the seeker. As the wood is seasoned, it may eventually catch flame. Rupert's teaching may be seen as the throwing off of numerous 'sparks' that progressively 'season' the seeker and lead – as with Plato – to the eventual kindling of unitive realisation.

The essence of non-dual understanding is summarised by Shankaracharya as, 'The Absolute is the only reality; the world is not in itself real; the individual self is not different from the Absolute'. In *Being Myself*, Rupert's focus is primarily on the concluding section of this statement, highlighting the essential identity between the individual 'I' and the Absolute 'I Am'. Everything that Rupert has to say in what follows is a pointer, a 'spark', to that essential insight.

The seemingly ordinary referent 'I' is a key to this realisation. What is this 'I'? Just as Ramana Maharshi repeatedly instructed seekers to enquire of themselves, 'Who am I?', so also the familiar question of Christ might be taken personally and directed inward: 'Who do you say I am?'

The words addressed to Moses from the theophany of the burning bush reply, 'I am that I Am', which may be understood as 'I Am is who I am'. The same answer may be found in al-Hallaj's ecstatic declaration, 'I am the Real', as well as in the 'great saying' of the Upanishads, 'I am the Absolute'.

Francis Bacon once observed that only some few books deserve to be thoroughly 'chewed and digested'. I would suggest that this is such a book. The process of hearing and reflecting is, for most seekers, gradual and protracted. The teaching is at once obvious and yet subtle; even when it is clearly grasped intellectually, the ego-sense remains persistent. Further, as much as Rupert's words are pointers, they are also, inescapably, veils. What he is gesturing towards is That for which we have no words and before which language fails. With patience, deep consideration and 'rumination', the veils of his words may eventually be pierced through and the reality shining behind and through them clearly recognised. May the reader find it so.

Peter Samsel
Ithaca, New York
September 2020

ACKNOWLEDGEMENTS

I would like to thank all those who have transcribed guided meditations from my live events, some of which form the basis of this book, in particular Ed Kelly, Leslie Tuchman, Monica Timbal, Michael Oliver, Annabelle Williams, Will Wright and Terri Bennett. I would also like to thank Jacqueline Boyle, Rob Bowden, Caroline Seymour, Kyra O'Keeffe, Linda Arzouni, Ruth Middleton, Stuart Moore and Peter Samsel, all of whom have contributed directly or indirectly to this publication and without whom it would not have come to pass. I am deeply grateful to them for their care, generosity and integrity.

The contemplations in this book are taken from guided meditations that Rupert Spira has given during meetings and retreats over the past several years. They were originally delivered spontaneously but have been edited for this collection to avoid repetition, and to adapt them from the spoken to the written word.

Meditation takes place in the space between words, although it remains present during the words themselves. Therefore, these contemplations were originally spoken with long silences between almost every sentence, allowing listeners time to explore the statements in their own experience. The meditations in this book have been laid out with numerous breaks between sentences and sections in order to invite and facilitate a similarly contemplative approach.

CHAPTER I

THE SENSE OF BEING MYSELF

Everyone has the sense of 'being myself'. The sense of 'being myself' is our most ordinary, intimate and familiar experience. It pervades all experience, irrespective of its content. It is the background of all experience.

The sense of 'being myself' never leaves us and cannot be separated from us.

If I am lonely, the sense of 'being myself' is present, although it is temporarily coloured by the feeling of loneliness. If I am in love, the sense of 'being myself' is present, although it is mixed with the feeling of being in love. The sense of 'being myself' is equally present in both feelings.

If I am tired, hungry, excited or in pain, the sense of 'being myself' remains present, albeit mixed with the experiences of tiredness, hunger, excitement or pain. Indeed, *all* experience is pervaded by the sense of 'being myself'.

Just as a screen is coloured by the images that appear on it, our knowledge of 'being myself' is qualified or conditioned by thoughts, feelings, sensations, perceptions, activities and relationships.

And just as the images change constantly but the screen remains the same, so experience changes all the time but the fact of 'being myself' is always the same.

'Being myself' is the ever-present factor in all changing experience.

* * *

Although we all have this sense of 'being myself', not everyone experiences their self *clearly*. In most cases, our sense of self is mixed up with the content of experience: thoughts, feelings, sensations, perceptions, activities and relationships.

There are, as such, two elements to our normal experience of self: our ever-present, unchanging being, and the qualities it derives from our constantly changing experience, which seem to condition and limit it.

All experience is limited by nature, and this mixture of self with the qualities of experience gives rise to a limited sense of self. This is the apparently separate self or ego on whose behalf most thoughts and feelings arise and in whose service most activities and relationships are undertaken.

Divested of the qualities of experience, our self has no characteristics and therefore no limitations of its own. It is simply unlimited or infinite being: transparent, empty, silent, still.

Sharing none of the agitation of our thoughts and feelings, our essential self or being is inherently peaceful. Just as the space of a room cannot be agitated by any of the people or objects within it, so our being cannot be disturbed by anything that takes place in experience.

In the absence of any inherent sense of lack, our being is naturally fulfilled, needing nothing from experience to complete itself, just as nothing in a movie adds anything to or takes anything away from the screen.

Thus, peace and happiness are the natural condition of our essential being, and they inform the thoughts, feelings, activities and relationships of one who knows their self clearly.

*   *   *

When we allow our essential self to become mixed or identified with the qualities of experience, its natural condition of peace and happiness is veiled or obscured.

Just as water has no taste of its own but assumes the taste of whatever it is mixed with and seems to become, for example, tea or coffee, so our essential self or being has no attributes of its own but assumes the qualities of experience and seems to become a person, a finite self or an ego.

For instance, when a feeling arises, such as sadness, loneliness or anxiety, we no longer know our self as we essentially are: transparent, silent, peaceful, fulfilled. Our knowledge of our self is mixed with and modified by the feeling. We overlook our being in favour of the feeling.

In fact, we seem to *become* the feeling. 'I *feel* sadness' becomes 'I *am* sad'. We lose our self in experience. We forget our self. However, this forgetting never completely eclipses the sense of 'being myself'. It is a partial veiling, for even in the darkest feelings we still have the experience of 'being myself'.

In depression, for instance, our experience is so coloured by darkness that our innate qualities of peace and happiness are almost completely obscured. Our self seems to be tarnished or darkened.

However, just as the nature of water stays the same even when mixed with tea or coffee, so our essential self remains in its pristine condition even when mixed with the content of experience. It is only necessary to stay in touch with one's essential self or being in the midst of all experience.

*   *   *

Feeling limited, the separate self or ego is prone to vulnerability and insecurity, and thus it seeks to defend itself. This is the impulse behind emotional reactivity: it is an attempt to restore the equilibrium that is the natural condition of our essential self or being.

Being vulnerable, the separate self or ego is inclined to feel unconfident, inferior and unloved, and in an attempt to re-establish the dignity inherent in our true nature, it seeks to aggrandise itself. This is the impulse behind most complaining, criticising and judging.

And feeling incomplete, the separate self or ego is given to a sense of insufficiency, inadequacy and unsatisfactoriness, and in an attempt to recover its natural condition of wholeness, it seeks fulfilment through the acquisition of objects, substances, activities, states of mind or relationships.

Thus, the separate self or ego lives in a constant state of lack: a chronic and pervasive sense of insufficiency punctuated by periods of acute distress. This suffering is the inevitable consequence of the overlooking or forgetting of our true self.

The depth of the suffering depends upon the extent of the amnesia, that is, the degree to which we allow the current feeling or experience to veil the peace and happiness at the core of our being.

Just as suffering is inevitable for the apparently separate self or ego, so resistance and seeking are the two activities that govern its thoughts, feelings, activities and relationships as it attempts to restore its innate peace and happiness.

Little does the separate self realise that what it truly longs for is not to defend or fulfil the entity it imagines itself to be, but to be divested of its apparent limitations and return to its natural condition.

*   *   *

This loss of peace and happiness initiates a great search in the realm of objective experience, which is destined sooner or later to fail. Indeed, none of us would be reading this book if the search had not, to a greater or lesser extent, failed.

Once we have become sufficiently disillusioned with the capacity of objective experience to provide the peace and happiness for which we long, many of us turn to religious or spiritual traditions, which seem to offer a promise of fulfilment.

To this end, we might devote ourself to meditation practices, prayer, yoga, visualisation, special diets, disciplined regimes and spiritual teachers. And these may, to some extent, relieve the pain of our longing and restore a degree of balance and harmony to our lives.

However, if our peace and happiness are dependent upon objective experience in any way, however refined or noble, we can be sure that underneath a veneer of peace, the sense of lack is smouldering. Sooner or later we must have the clarity and courage to return from the adventure of experience and come back to our self.

The great secret that lies at the heart of all the main religious and spiritual traditions is the understanding that the peace and happiness for which all people long can never be delivered via objective experience. It can only be found in our self, in the depths of our being.

*   *   *

The separate self or ego is the apparent entity that arises from the intermingling of our self with the limitations of experience. The divesting of our being of the qualities it seems to have acquired from experience is referred to as 'enlightenment' in the traditional literature. Our being sheds the limitations of experience that seemed to obscure or 'endarken' it.

Enlightenment is, as such, not a new or extraordinary experience to be attained or acquired; it is simply the revelation of the original nature of our self or being. Nothing could be more intimate and familiar than our being, which is why it feels like coming home. In the Zen tradition it is referred to as the recognition of our original face.

There is nothing exotic or mystical about enlightenment. It is simply the recognition of something that was always known, indeed *is* always known, before it is clouded by experience.

8

No one *becomes* enlightened. Our being is simply relieved of an imaginary limitation and, as a result, its natural condition of peace and happiness shines.

CHAPTER 2

OUR NAKED BEING

The essence of anything is that which cannot be separated from it. No thought, image, feeling, sensation, perception, activity or relationship is essential to us, just as no movie is integral to the screen on which it appears.

Experiences, like movies, come and go. Our essential self, however, never appears or disappears. It is ever-present and unchanging. It is the one constant factor in all changing experience.

When we are divested of the qualities and limitations we acquire from experience, only that which is intrinsic to us, our naked, unconditioned being, remains. In fact, we cannot even call it *our* being, for without limitations it is no longer coloured by the characteristics of a person.

It is our innermost essence and is, at the same time, utterly impersonal: intimate, impersonal, infinite being.

Being is not a quality or an attribute belonging to a person. A person is a temporary name and form of intimate, impersonal, infinite being.

It is this impersonal, infinite being that shines in each of us as the sense of 'being myself' before it is qualified by experience.

Divested of the qualities it inherits from experience, being is infinite, perfect, whole and indivisible, and all people, animals and things borrow their apparently independent existence from it.

This unity of being shines in each of our minds as the sense of 'being myself' or the knowledge 'I am'. It shines in the world as the 'is-ness' of things.

The recognition of our shared being is the experience of love in relation to people and animals, and beauty in relation to objects and the world.

*   *   *

All thoughts and feelings, irrespective of their content, whether they are pleasant, unpleasant or neutral, arise and pass away. Even our most intimate and treasured feelings are not always present, and something that is not always with us cannot be essential to us.

For this reason, there is never any need to manipulate or get rid of any thought or feeling, but only to see clearly that our essential self or being is prior to and independent of thoughts and feelings. Our essential self has no need to be *made* independent through effort or practice. It is always and already inherently free. It is only necessary to recognise it as such.

Whatever the character of any bodily sensation, none are present continuously; sensations are always appearing, evolving and disappearing in our experience. We do not therefore need to manipulate our experience of the body in any way. It is only necessary to recognise that our being is prior to and independent of the condition of the body.

The same is true of our perceptions of the world: sights, sounds, tastes, textures and smells. All of these appear, exist, evolve and vanish. None are essential to us.

Furthermore, no relationship is essential to us. No matter how intimate, none are indispensable. In fact, without reference to thought in this moment, one would have no knowledge of having or being in a relationship. This does not imply that relationship is not valid or desirable but simply that our essential self or being is prior to and independent of it.

Nor is any activity essential to us. Everything we do is pervaded by the sense of 'being myself'. As we engage in an activity we may become completely absorbed in or identified with it, but when it stops, our self or being simply remains as it always is.

Nothing ever happens to pure being.

*.   *   *

What remains when we have let go of all thoughts, images, memories, feelings, sensations, perceptions, activities and relationships?

Our self alone remains: not an enlightened, higher, spiritual, special self or a self that we have *become* through effort, practice or discipline, but just the essential self or being that we always and already are before it is coloured by experience.

We are not manipulating experience; we are simply contemplating it. Nor is our self evolving. It is simply being seen clearly without the limitations it seems to have acquired from experience.

Being is always in the same pristine condition. If we refer now to the feeling of 'being myself' before it is coloured by experience, and if we were to have visited the same experience at the age of five, ten, twenty or thirty, we would always have found the *same* self, the same unqualified being.

Nothing happens to our being throughout the vicissitudes of life. Its nature is never tarnished or diminished by experience. It has simply been temporarily obscured.

It's like undressing before going to bed at night. We take off everything that can be removed, and our naked body remains. Our naked body is not created each time by undressing; it is simply revealed.

Nor do we *become* our naked body when we take our clothes off; it was present throughout the day, though we may not have noticed it, covered as it was by layers of clothing.

We return to our naked being in a similar way. In fact, we do not *return* to our being, because we never truly left it. Our being never leaves itself. We take our being with us wherever we go; it is present in whatever we think, feel or do.

We simply 'undress'. That is, we see clearly that our being lies beneath or behind all experience.

*   *   *

Divested of the qualities it borrows from experience, our essential self or being is unconditioned and unlimited. Having no objective qualities, it cannot be defined or described in terms which have evolved to convey the content of objective experience, for all such language is tinged, to a greater or lesser extent, with the limitations inherent in this objectivity.

The best we can do to describe a screen, which has no colour of its own, is to say what it is *not* – not blue, not red, not green, not yellow – rather than what it *is*, and words such as 'transparent', 'colourless' and 'empty' are simply attempts to convey this.

So if we are to speak of our essential self or being, we have no choice but to make a concession and borrow words from ordinary language: 'transparent', 'spacious', 'silent', 'still', 'peaceful' and 'fulfilled' are meant to evoke the qualities of our essential being rather than describe it, though even to suggest that our essential being has any qualities at all is itself a concession.

Our thoughts may be agitated, but in their absence, and even in their background when they are present, our essential self is devoid of any such quality. This absence of agitation is referred to as 'peace', and thus peace is said to be inherent in our being.

We may feel a sense of lack, but prior to and in the background of any such feeling, our essential self knows no lack, and we call the absence of lack 'happiness'. Thus, our being is said to be happiness itself.

The terms 'peace' and 'happiness' do not describe feelings or emotions in the normal sense of the words. They are the very *nature* of our self in the absence of the limitations we seem to acquire from experience.

As soon as our self or being disentangles itself from the adventure of experience and 'returns' to itself, it recognises or tastes itself again as it essentially is. That taste is happiness itself.

*   *   *

Just as an actor dresses up, assumes the thoughts and feelings of a character in a play and seems to *become* that character, without ever actually ceasing to be an actor, so our essential being clothes itself in the qualities of experience and seems to become a temporary, finite self, without ever actually ceasing to be eternal, infinite awareness.

Imagine an actor named John Smith who is playing the part of King Lear. John Smith leads a peaceful and fulfilled life. Every night he leaves home, goes to the theatre, puts on his costume and adopts King Lear's thoughts and feelings.

One night, the play begins as usual and King Lear starts arguing with his daughters. But as the play develops, he becomes increasingly involved in the drama, to such an extent that at some point he forgets that he is John Smith and seems actually to become King Lear. John Smith believes and feels 'I am King Lear'. The moment that thought and feeling take hold of him, his suffering begins.

The play comes to an end but he forgets to revert to John Smith, so lost is he in the drama of experience. When a friend comes to his dressing room to congratulate him, he finds King Lear miserable. 'Why are you miserable?' his friend enquires. 'That was wonderful!'

King Lear responds, 'I'm miserable because of my relationship with Cordelia and the war with France'.

Understanding his predicament, his friend says, 'No, you are miserable because you have forgotten who you are. Who are you really?' King Lear replies, 'I'm the father of three daughters and the King of England'.

'No, no. That's not who you really are!' his friend exclaims. 'Who are you *before* you are a father or a king? Go back, deeper into yourself.'

So King Lear starts describing his thoughts and feelings, and again his friend says, 'No, these thoughts and feelings are not essential to you. They are not always with you. Who are you *prior to* your thoughts and feelings?'

King Lear goes deeper and deeper into himself, discarding his relationships, activities, thoughts, feelings, history and conditioning, until everything that is not essential to him has gone and he stands revealed, unqualified by any experience. Very quietly he says, 'I am John Smith'. At that moment, his suffering disappears.

*   *   *

Just as the recognition 'I am John Smith' is the revelation of King Lear's essential self, the clear seeing of our naked being is the recognition of our self – not something we once knew but have since forgotten, but the recollection of something that is present *now* and *always* known but usually ignored or overlooked.

It is the revelation of our essential, irreducible nature before it is obscured by experience, and with this revelation, peace and happiness are restored.

In fact, everyone knows their own being, or has the experience of 'being myself', at every moment of experience. No one's knowledge of their self can ever be completely obscured by the content of experience. Even in our darkest moments we still have the sense of 'being myself'. The sense of 'being myself' never leaves us, because it *is* us and we cannot leave our self.

Everything apart from our self may take its leave of us, but our self cannot leave itself, just as, relatively speaking, we cannot step out of our body. We can step out of our clothes, but not our body.

Just as we take our naked body with us wherever we go, even though it is usually covered by clothes, so we take our naked being with us whatever we do, even though it is usually obscured by experience.

And just as it is not necessary to undress in order to feel our naked body, it is not necessary to change the content of experience in any way in order to be in touch with our innate peace and happiness.

CHAPTER 3

We refer to ourself throughout our life as 'I': 'I am twenty-four, forty-five or sixty-eight years old', 'I am five feet four or six feet two', 'I am French or English', 'I am healthy or sick', 'I am rich or poor', 'I am lonely or unhappy', 'I am tired or cold', 'I am single or married', 'I am a mother or a father', 'I am a doctor or an artist', 'I am walking down the street', 'I am reading a book', and so on.

In each of these statements we refer to our essential self – 'I' or 'I am' – which is consistently present throughout all experience, and which is qualified by various changing feelings, states, conditions, activities or relationships.

I am not always twenty-four, forty-five or sixty-eight years old, but I always *am*. I am not always five feet four or six feet two, but I always am. I am not always lonely, unhappy, tired or cold, but I always am. I am not always single or in a relationship, but I always am. I am not always walking down the street or reading a book, but I always am.

I am not always any of these things in particular, but I always am. All feelings, states, conditions, activities or relationships are added to me and then removed from me. They are not part of what I essentially am. They are not part of my essential being.

Our essential self or being shines in each of us as the sense of 'being myself', the feeling of being or the pure knowledge 'I am'. This knowledge is described as pure because, before becoming qualified by the content of experience, it is devoid of any objective quality. It is transparent, empty, silent and at peace.

* * *

It is on account of its transparency or emptiness that a screen is able to display innumerable colours. When it is coloured by an image, its original, transparent 'nature' does not disappear; it is just temporarily qualified by that colour. When the colour fades away, nothing new happens to the screen; it simply loses a temporary shade and its natural transparent condition is revealed.

Just as the screen seems to acquire the colours it displays, our self seems to acquire the qualities of experience: 'I am' seems to become 'I am this' or 'I am that'. But just as no colour is inherent in the screen, no attribute or quality is intrinsic to our self. When we are divested of the various qualities we acquire from experience, all that remains is naked, aware being.

However, our self or being is too close to itself to be known as an objective experience, just as the eyes cannot see themselves. The eyes can only see something that is at a distance from them and, similarly, our self can only know something at an apparent distance from itself. We cannot separate our self from our self in order to know it as an object of experience.

At the same time, our own being is not something unknown or unfamiliar to us. In fact, our own being is more intimately known to us than anything else. Our own being is closer to us than our most intimate thoughts and feelings. For this reason, we do not have to go anywhere or do anything special in order to be aware of our self.

If someone were to ask us now to stand up and take a step towards ourself, where would we go? What would we do?

Could we go anywhere that would take us closer to ourself? And could we go anywhere that would take us farther away?

It is the same with our being: where do we have to go, or what do we have to do, to be aware of our own being? The fact of being aware is not something we can get closer to or farther from. Being aware, or aware being, is what we always *are*, irrespective of the content of experience.

If anything, it would be more accurate to suggest that we *cease* doing something, that is, cease allowing our self to become obscured by the content of experience. Once we have seen that our self or being is not qualified by experience, nothing need be done; it shines by itself.

* * *

Unqualified, unconditioned aware being shines in each of our minds as the knowledge 'I' or 'I am'. It is the feeling of being or the sense of 'being myself', before it has been coloured or qualified by experience.

Aware being is not something extraordinary or unfamiliar. It is the self in all selves, the being in all beings. It cannot be lost or found. But it can be veiled and then recognised. When John Smith dresses up in King Lear's clothes and adopts his thoughts and feelings, he assumes their qualities and limitations and seems, as a result, to become the character King Lear. As such, King Lear is John Smith plus an imaginary limitation, although in reality John Smith is always only John Smith.

When King Lear feels 'I, myself', the 'I' that he is feeling is John Smith, the only 'I' there is. That is, the self of John Smith shines in King Lear's experience as the knowledge 'I' or 'I am'.

It is in fact not King Lear who knows himself as 'I', for the only self or person present in King Lear is John Smith. King Lear's knowledge 'I' is John Smith's knowledge of himself.

King Lear's problem is that he does not see himself, John Smith, clearly. Or rather, John Smith's knowledge of himself is so obscured by King Lear's thoughts and feelings that he does not know himself as he is and thus loses touch with his innate peace and happiness.

All King Lear's experience is temporary, finite and conditioned, apart from one aspect: the pure feeling 'I'. This is the only element of his experience that has nothing to do with the character King Lear.

In order to recognise his true nature and taste its inherent peace and happiness, King Lear does not need to explore his thoughts, feelings, activities and relationships but simply to go to that pure feeling of 'I, myself' or the knowledge 'I am'.

Likewise, instead of emphasising the content of experience and allowing our essential self or being to fade into the background, all that is necessary is to allow the content of experience to recede and allow being to emerge.

* * *

Our self or being, which shines in each of us as the knowledge 'I am', is the constant factor in all changing experience.

If I am depressed, I am present there. If I am lonely, tired or in love, I am present there. If I am drinking tea or walking down the street, I am present there. Whatever I am thinking, feeling, perceiving or doing, I am present.

Our essential being shines equally in all experience, irrespective of its content. Even our darkest feelings shine brightly with the light of being. All that is necessary is to give attention to being in the midst of experience, before it is qualified or conditioned by it.

However, we are not one thing and our self or being another, to which we can direct our attention, as we might direct attention to a thought or a perception. We *are* our self or being.

It is our self, the simple fact of being aware or awareness itself, that directs its attention away from itself, towards the content of experience, thereby ignoring or overlooking itself. And it is our self that disentangles itself from the content of experience and returns to itself.

*　*　*

If someone were to ask us to be aware of the sound of the wind or traffic, the sensation at the soles of our feet or the view from our window, we would direct our attention towards each of these. But if someone were to suggest being aware of *our self*, what would we do with our attention?

The word 'attention' comes from two Latin words, *ad*, meaning 'to' or 'towards', and *tendere*, meaning 'to stretch'. Just as the sun shines its light on the earth but cannot shine it on itself, because it is too close to itself, so we can focus on or 'stretch' our attention towards an object of experience but we cannot do the same towards our self. There is no distance, and therefore no pathway, from our self to our self.

If anything, all that is required is to relax the focus of attention from its objective content and allow it to flow back to its source. Our self lies at the *source* of attention; it can never be its object. It is by resting or relaxing our attention that the recognition of our self is accomplished, never by directing or disciplining it.

We cannot become what we are; we cannot be what we are not. Therefore, in this approach, meditation is not considered an activity that is undertaken by the mind; it is the very nature of our self. Meditation is what we *are*, not what we *do*.

The simple fact of being shines in each of us as the knowledge 'I' or 'I am'. All that is necessary is to turn towards it and it will take us into itself.

*　*　*

In the Old Testament, God appeared to Moses in the burning bush, and when Moses asked Him who He was, God is said to have replied, 'I am that I am'. I am the awareness that is aware that I am.

It is a simple and profound statement of our essential identity. And in case Moses' words seem enigmatic, Popeye expressed the same understanding: 'I am what I am and that's all that

I am'. He realised that his essential being shares none of the qualities of experience but remains intact throughout all changing experience, unmodified, unfragmented and unqualified.

If properly understood, these statements convey the essential truth at the heart of all the great religious and spiritual traditions, and indicate where the peace and happiness for which we long above all else are to be found. It is only the extent to which the knowledge of our self is veiled by the content of experience that accounts for the varying degrees of peace and happiness we feel.

Being is not something that some people have more of than others, nor does anyone have privileged access to it. The unqualified, unconditioned aware being that shone clearly in Moses, the Buddha, Jesus, Meister Eckhart, Ramana Maharshi and many others as the knowledge 'I' or 'I am', the feeling of being or simply the sense of 'being myself' is exactly the same aware being that shines presently in each of us.

The only difference is that their essential being was not eclipsed by the content of experience. Experience had lost its capacity to take them away from themselves.

*   *   *

Divested of the qualities it derives from experience, our self is without personal characteristics or attributes, for all such traits are derived from personal experience.

Our essential self is thus impersonal, and yet it is utterly intimate. It both transcends experience and is immanent within it. There is no aspect of experience that is not pervaded by the sense of our self or being. At the same time, our self or being does not share the limits or destiny of anything that takes place in experience.

In just the same way, the space in a room pervades the room but is not limited to or contained by it. The space is unlimited; our being is likewise infinite. It is not, in fact, *our* being but simply *being*, for being is not the attribute of a person, any more than space is the property of a room.

The being that shines in each of our minds as 'I' or 'I am' is not a personal being or self. It is the single, infinite, indivisible, impersonal being, refracted into numerous apparent selves without ever becoming fragmented. We all share the same being.

In religious terms, this single, infinite, indivisible, impersonal being is said to be sacred, for it shares none of the limited qualities of human experience, although it is the very essence of a human being.

All the qualities we most admire in a human being are those that are an expression of the nature of our essential self or being. It is the divine in us that makes us truly human.

CHAPTER 4

OUR SELF IS THE KNOWING ELEMENT
IN ALL EXPERIENCE

What is it that knows or is aware of our experience? Allow the question to take you from whatever you are aware of to that which knows or is aware.

The suggestion that this question could 'take us to' that which knows or is aware unintentionally implies that we are an entity and 'that which knows or is aware' is something we can approach.

We *are* awareness! We cannot be taken there; we cannot go there. I cannot go towards myself because I already *am* myself.

So when we ask what it is that knows or is aware of our experience, it is we, as awareness, who cease directing our attention towards the objective content of our experience – thoughts, images, feelings, sensations and perceptions –

and come back to our self. We remember our self. We become aware of our self.

In fact, we are always aware of our self, for being aware is what we *are*, not what we *do*. Awareness shines at the very heart of everyone's experience, even if, in most cases, it is veiled by experience.

*   *   *

Even when apparently veiled by the content of experience, awareness's knowledge of itself filters through experience as the sense of 'being myself'.

The sense of 'being myself' lies at the heart of all experience, pervading it intimately, irrespective of its content. Whatever we are thinking, feeling or perceiving, each of us is now having the experience of 'being myself'.

What is it that has the experience of 'being myself'? Whatever it is must itself be aware. If it were not, it would not be aware of the experience of 'being myself', or indeed any other experience. It is I, awareness, who have the experience of 'being myself'.

The experience of 'being myself' is awareness's knowledge of itself. It is not a person's knowledge of their self, for a person is not itself aware. Only awareness is aware, and awareness is not an attribute of a person.

A person is a collection of thoughts, images, feelings, sensations and perceptions. Each of these is an *object* of experience that we, awareness, are *aware of*.

A thought is not aware it is a thought. It does not have the subjective experience of 'being myself' and therefore never calls itself 'I'; likewise a feeling or perception. No object of experience can know its own existence.

And yet each of us undoubtedly has the experience 'I am'. Only that which knows itself has the experience 'I am'. Only awareness knows itself and can therefore have the experience of 'being myself' or 'I am'. Only awareness knows its own existence.

'I' is the name that anything that knows itself gives to itself. Therefore, the name 'I' or the knowledge 'I am' refers only to awareness's knowledge of itself. Our knowledge of our self *is* awareness's knowledge of itself.

*   *   *

Awareness's knowledge of itself is its primary knowledge. Just as the sun illuminates itself before anything else, so awareness is aware of itself before it is aware of any other thing.

The sun does not have to make any effort to illuminate itself but does so simply by being itself; self-illumination is its nature. Illumination is what it *is*, not what it *does*. Likewise, awareness is effortlessly self-aware; being aware of itself is its natural condition, not something it does from time to time.

We, awareness, know our self simply by being our self. Most of the time, however, we are accustomed to directing our attention away from our self towards the objective content of experience, and in the process we overlook or forget our self. In order to know our self we must simply come back to our self.

This return to our being from the adventure of experience may seem, from the point of view of the person, to require an effort, but in fact it is the cessation or relaxation of an effort of which we were previously unaware. It is the relaxation of the tension in attention.

* * *

In order to know that I am, the mind does not need to be in any particular condition. No special circumstances are necessary, nor is any preparation required. The knowledge 'I am' is not sophisticated or mysterious. It is the most ordinary, intimate and familiar experience there is.

Everybody can say from their own direct experience, 'I know that I am', irrespective of the condition of their mind or body, or whatever is taking place in their environment.

It is our *experience* that I am. 'I am' refers to our knowledge of our self before it is qualified by experience. Before we know that I am a man or a woman, of such-and-such an age, married or single, a mother, father or friend, before we know anything about our self, we simply know that I am.

Before we know *what* I am, we know *that* I am. Everything we know about our self is added to the simple knowledge 'I am'.

If we feel that our self is not clearly known as it essentially is, it is not because we do not know it but because we have forgotten or ignored it in favour of objective experience. We have become so accustomed to giving our love and attention to the content of experience that we have simply overlooked that which is closest and most familiar to us.

To remedy this, we first make a distinction between the knower and the known, the experiencer and the experienced, the witness and the witnessed. Later on we will collapse this distinction, but for one who is lost in experience, who identifies with every passing thought, feeling, activity and relationship, it is first necessary to make the distinction.

We are the knowing element in all changing knowledge and experience. All experience happens to us, is known by us or appears within us, but we are not any particular experience.

*　　*　　*

'I' is the word that everybody uses to indicate that which knows or is aware of their experience; it is pure knowing or being aware.

Pure knowing is knowing that has no objective content. Whatever it is that knows our thoughts is itself inherently free of all thoughts. Whatever it is that is aware of our feelings and sensations is itself prior to and independent of all feeling and sensation. Whatever it is that knows sights, sounds, tastes, textures and smells is itself free of all seeing, hearing, tasting, touching and smelling. It is thus sometimes said to be empty.

'Empty' in this context just means empty of objective content, rather than a blank or void. It is empty of objects but full of pure knowing, full of awareness. This pure knowing or empty awareness that we refer to as 'I' is our essential, irreducible self.

Our self is said to be essential because it is that which cannot be removed from us. No thought, image, feeling, perception, activity or relationship is continuously present. Only the experience of being aware remains with us all the time. In fact, it does not remain *with* us, as if it were one thing and we another; it *is* what we essentially are.

Our self is said to be irreducible because we cannot go further back in our experience than being aware. All experience dissolves into being aware or awareness, but awareness itself never dissolves into anything.

Being aware or aware being is ever-present. No experience qualifies, conditions, changes, moves or harms it. There is never any more or less of it. It cannot be enhanced or diminished. It cannot grow old, tired, sick or lonely. It is always in the same pristine, ageless, thought-less, feeling-less, gender-less condition.

It is sometimes referred to as the unconditioned or original mind, the mind before it has been conditioned by experience. It is pure consciousness, consciousness without form or objective attributes. Its common name is simply 'I'.

In time it will become clear, if it is not already, that this knowledge of our own being, its knowledge of itself, is not only the most profound knowledge possible but also the most precious. It is the source of the peace and happiness for which we long above all else, and the foundation for the resolution of all conflicts.

CHAPTER 5

THE NATURE OF OUR SELF

All experience arises within us, within awareness. We are like an aware screen upon which the movie of experience is playing and with which it is known.

Just as the screen never appears as an object in the movie, we never appear as an object in or of experience. We can never be found or known as a thought, image, feeling, sensation or perception.

And just as the screen is neither separate from the movie nor limited by it, we are not separate from experience, nor are we limited or conditioned by it.

We are the colourless, unlimited, unconditioned, self-aware screen upon which all experience plays, with which all experience is known and, ultimately, out of which all experience is made. All experience is made of our self, but our self is not made of any particular experience. Experience is the activity of awareness.

This awareness is not a spiritual, metaphysical or enlightened awareness to which only certain special people have privileged access. It is the ordinary, intimate, familiar awareness with which each of us is currently aware of our experience, to which we refer when we say 'I' or 'myself'.

Nor is this a description of how we might *become* if we meditate for long enough or practise hard enough. It is simply an attempt, within the limitations of language, to describe or evoke the presence of awareness as it is now and has always been: intimately one with all experience but sharing none of its qualities; unconditioned, unlimited, infinite.

*   *   *

The awareness that knows our current experience is not different from that which knew our experience ten minutes, ten days or ten years ago. Our thoughts, sensations and perceptions change constantly, but awareness itself has not changed.

As a child we looked at the ocean and said, 'I see the water'. Now we look around and say, 'I see the room'. The water and the room are different, but it is the same awareness that perceived the water then and perceives the room now.

Throughout the adventure of our lives, we have not changed or aged. We are always in the same pristine, ageless condition.

Nothing ever happens to awareness. It is never changed, moved or harmed by any experience, just as a screen is never stained or tarnished by the content of a movie. Awareness is always in the same transparent, luminous, spacious, welcoming condition.

And just as nothing that takes place in a movie adds or removes anything from the screen, nothing that takes place in experience adds or removes anything from our essential nature of pure awareness. We are never aggrandised or diminished by experience.

We are always perfect, whole, complete and inherently fulfilled. We never gain or lose anything from the drama of experience. The drama only turns into trauma when we get lost in it or become identified with it.

*   *   *

Unqualified, unconditioned aware being shines in each of our minds as the knowledge 'I' or 'I am', the feeling of simply being or the sense of 'being myself', before what I am has been mixed with or coloured by experience. What is the nature of our self before it is qualified by experience?

I am and I know that I am. In that simple knowing of our own being there is no experience of having an age. In order to believe that we have an age, it is necessary to refer to thought. In the absence of thinking, we have no experience of age.

Even in the presence of thinking, there may be the belief in time but never the actual experience of time. There is just the current experience, appearing now. Age is never an experience; it is always a concept.

Without reference to thought or memory, we have no actual experience of having a gender. Gender is an interpretation of sensations and perceptions; it is not an experience. None of these are essential to us and, therefore, none qualify what we essentially are.

The gender-fluidity movement originates from the intuition that our essential self or being has no gender, even if, in most cases, the separate self has appropriated this understanding and used it to perpetuate its illusory identity in a different guise.

Referring only to the knowing of being, there is no experience of shape, size or weight. These are also derived from sensations and perceptions. They do not give us any knowledge of our self.

In the pure knowledge 'I am' there is no experience of age, gender, shape, size, weight, nationality, location, solidity, density or history. Before the 'I am' is mixed with the content of experience, it has no form and therefore cannot legitimately be named. And yet it is our self.

*   *   *

We are the awareness with which sensations and perceptions are known, in which they appear and, ultimately, out of which they are made.

It is only when we allow our essential self to become mixed with sensations and perceptions, and interpreted by thought, that we seem to become qualified by and limited to them.

If we stay close to the evidence of experience, that is, close to the knowledge of our self, we experience no form within our self. We are simply formless awareness. Even to say that is to say too much, but if we are to say anything at all about this, we must allow some concession to language.

If awareness relaxes its attention from the objective content of experience, its awareness of itself emerges from obscurity in the background of experience.

Awareness is without form and, therefore, has no limit. Just as the space of a room fills the room but is not limited by it, so awareness pervades the body but is not confined by it.

Just as the space of the room is not generated by the four walls, nor does it share their destiny, so awareness is not generated by the body and nor does it share its destiny. In awareness's experience of itself, there is no knowledge of birth or death.

* * *

No experience leaves a trace on awareness and nothing can harm, modify or destroy it. Therefore, it is without fear. As the space of a room cannot be agitated by anything that takes place within it, so awareness cannot be disturbed by anything that occurs in experience. Thus, our nature is peace.

And just as nothing that takes place inside a room adds anything to the space, nothing that takes place in experience adds anything to our self. We are inherently and unconditionally fulfilled. Thus, in the experience of happiness we taste or know our true nature. It knows itself as it essentially is.

In the Vedantic tradition this understanding is expressed by the simple phrase *sat chit ananda*. *Sat* means 'being', *chit* 'knowledge' or 'consciousness', and *ananda* 'peace' or 'happiness'. Thus, *sat chit ananda* means 'To know your own being is happiness itself', or, put more simply, 'You *are* happiness itself'.

The experience of happiness is our being shining in the midst of experience. That is all anybody ever truly seeks; we are simply seeking our own being. Our being is seeking to come back to itself, to know or taste itself again, to recognise itself.

Peace and happiness are not experiences that happen to us from time to time or that alternate with agitation and suffering. They may be eclipsed by the content of experience, but they are never absent.

Peace and happiness are not even *qualities of* our self; they simply *are* our self. Every time we experience peace or happiness, we are experiencing the shining of our own being.

CHAPTER 6

THE MEMORY OF OUR ETERNITY

How might we turn the understanding of our ever-present, unconditioned and unlimited nature into our actual felt experience?

Imagine the physical space of a room, and add the quality of awareness to it. It is now an *aware* physical space, a *knowing* space. And now imagine that the aware physical space were to investigate its experience.

If it directed its attention to the objects in the room, it would always find them appearing and disappearing. Even the four walls which seemed to contain it would appear and disappear in its experience. However, the aware physical space would have no experience of its *own* appearance or disappearance. In its own experience of itself it would be ever-present and unlimited.

If we now remove the space-like quality from this compound of space and awareness, all that remains is dimensionless awareness. That is our self.

We, awareness, have the experience of the appearance and disappearance of the sensations and perceptions that constitute our knowledge of the body and world, but we never have the experience of the appearance or disappearance of *our self.*

We have no knowledge of coming into being with the appearance of the body or of ceasing to exist when the sensations and perceptions that constitute the experience of the body disappear.

We cannot even say that we existed before the body or will continue after its death. Before the body there is no 'before' and after the death of the body there is no 'after'. Even during the existence of the body there is no time present in which awareness endures.

We are not everlasting in time; we are ever-present now. We are eternal. Jesus indicated this when he said, 'Before Abraham was, I am'.*

*　　*　　*

* Gospel of John, 8:59.

Return to our aware physical space and imagine it taking three samples of itself: one, five hundred years ago, before the building it now fills was erected; two, now; and three, in five hundred years' time, after the building has been demolished.

If the aware space were now to compare the three samples of itself, it would find them all identical. Nothing that took place during the thousand-year period of the experiment would have affected it in any way. It would not have aged, deteriorated or become tarnished. It would always remain in the same pristine condition.

Now return to our experience of our self. If we were to sample our thoughts, feelings, sensations and perceptions at various stages of our life, each would be different. But if, at various ages, we were to sample our *self*, our naked being before it is qualified by experience, we would find it always in the same pristine condition.

Our self never experiences any change in itself. Divested of the qualities it acquires from experience, it is simply present and aware, colouring itself in all forms of experience but never being or becoming anything other than itself.

Nothing ever happens to our self!

*   *   *

Imagine that the aware physical space were to look around itself at the objects in the room. Everything it saw would be limited. But if the aware space no longer gave its attention to the objects in the room and allowed its awareness to come back to itself, it would not find any limit there.

It would find an edge to all the objects in the room, but none to itself. It would find itself open, empty, spacious.

Likewise, we find a limit in either time or space to everything that we know objectively, but we find no limit in our self. Even time and space are objects of experience, for they appear and disappear in awareness.

In fact, time and space are never actually experienced. In the absence of thought there is no experience of time, and in the absence of perception there is no experience of space.

Even in the *presence* of thought and perception there is no actual experience of time and space. Time is *deduced* from thought, and space from perception.

This is confirmed every night when we fall deeply asleep. In the absence of thought and perception there is no experience of time or space: they are how the eternal, infinite nature of awareness appears when it is filtered through the prism of thought and perception.

In our own experience of our self, we, awareness, are unlimited or infinite. We do not become unlimited or infinite through effort, practice or discipline. We simply recognise our self as such.

This recognition is not an extraordinary, mystical experience. It is simply the recognition of the nature of our self or being as it is now.

* * *

Sometimes it is said in the traditional literature that our self, the presence of awareness, 'transcends' experience. This is a true but somewhat misleading idea that suggests that our self is *beyond* experience and thus mysterious, unreachable and unknowable.

It is true that our self cannot know itself as an object of experience. At the same time, it never ceases to know itself, just as the sun never ceases to illuminate itself.

Our self does not transcend experience in the sense of being beyond it; it is *prior to* experience. Awareness lies *behind* and is present *in the midst of* all experience.

John Smith does not lie beyond King Lear, at an infinite distance from him. He is the very essence of King Lear. Nothing could be more intimate, familiar and well known to King Lear than John Smith. Even King Lear's most intimate thoughts and feelings are like strangers to him compared with the intimacy of the presence of John Smith.

Describing our self as 'infinite' and 'eternal' may seem to imply that it is at a vast distance from the very ordinary, intimate, familiar self that we know as 'myself'. Nothing could be more misleading.

'Infinite', when used in relation to our essential self, simply means that our self does not share the limitations of experience, just as the space of a room shares none of the limitations of the objects within it, and John Smith shares none of the limitations of King Lear's thoughts and feelings.

Likewise, 'eternal' does not imply that our self resides in some mysterious dimension of which we have no experience. It just means that whilst all thoughts, images, feelings, sensations and perceptions continually appear and disappear, our essential self or being remains present throughout.

Our essential self is the ever-present factor in all temporary, changing experience. It does not exist on the horizontal dimension of time. It is the vertical dimension of being.

*　　*　　*

Our essential self does not share the qualities or limits of thoughts, feelings, sensations and perceptions and is, therefore, impersonal. Yet it is, at the same time, utterly intimate.

The self pervades the body but is not located in or qualified by it. It does not share the limits or destiny of the body any more than space shares the limits or destiny of the building in which it seems to be contained. It is intimate, impersonal and infinite.

This intimate, impersonal, infinite self or 'I' is the only 'I' there is. In religious language it is referred to as God's presence. God's presence does not shine *in* an individual self, for there is no such separate, individual self within which to shine. John Smith does not live *in* King Lear, for King Lear is simply an apparent limitation *of* John Smith.

There is no personal self whose essence is impersonal and universal. There is no higher or lower, enlightened or un-enlightened self. There is just the intimate, impersonal, infinite self, which becomes temporarily mixed with the qualities of experience and seems, as a result, to become temporary and finite, without ever actually ceasing to be itself.

The self of every self is God's infinite, self-aware being, the only self there is. The being we know as our self *is* God's being – in fact, not even God's being, as if being were an attribute of an entity called God. Infinite being is not an attribute of anyone or anything.

There is only intimate, impersonal, infinite, self-aware being. It is referred to as God in the religious traditions, awareness or consciousness in spiritual circles and, in ordinary language, 'I'.

The person who embarks on a search for happiness, enlightenment or God is like King Lear travelling the world in search of John Smith. They are looking for their own being. The experience of happiness, the light of being or God's presence shines in each of us as the knowledge 'I am', the sense of 'being myself' or simply the feeling of being.

One who turns towards their own being will be divested, usually gradually but occasionally suddenly, of all their acquired limitations and will, sooner or later, stand revealed as infinite, impersonal, self-aware being. That is the essence of prayer or meditation.

*   *   *

The name 'I' or the knowledge 'I am' refers to the element of experience that is unchanging and unchangeable. It is open, without resistance, to all experience and yet cannot be harmed. It is never enhanced or diminished by any particular experience, however pleasant or unpleasant.

Our being is always in the same pristine condition. It does not need to be purified or perfected. It never appears and disappears; it does not move or change. It does not grow old, sick or tired. All experience is added to it and removed from it, but its basic nature never changes. Being never disappears or dies.

Being is indivisible: it cannot be divided into objects and selves. Everything and everyone borrows its apparently independent existence from it, without ever actually becoming an object or an entity in its own right.

This impersonal, unlimited, indestructible, indivisible, self-aware being fills our body as the feeling of 'being myself' and shines in the mind as the knowledge 'I am'. It shines in the world as the is-ness of things.

The being in all beings is the *same* being. We share our being. Perception refracts impersonal, infinite, indivisible being into an apparent multiplicity and diversity of objects and selves, and thought gives them their names.

Love is the experience of our shared being. When we love another person we feel, to a greater or lesser extent, that the separation between us dissolves.

Love is not a relationship. It is a vertical intervention of reality into the horizontal dimension of time, which is characterised by the subject–object relationship. Love is the collapse of this relationship. It is the end of the apparently separate self or person. It is the taste of eternity.

When we long to love or to be loved, we long not for the person or the relationship but to be divested of everything that makes us feel separate, temporary, limited and confined. We long for the freedom of our true nature. We long to return to our original, unlimited being.

We long for love above all else, because the memory of eternity shines in each of our minds, irrespective of the extent to which it may be veiled by experience. Indeed, our longing is love itself filtering through this veil.

We all long to be returned to our original nature, whether we realise it or not. All that is necessary is to take the thought 'I' or the feeling of 'being myself' and allow it to draw us inwards, as if the self were constantly saying to itself, 'Turn towards me and I will take you into myself'.

CHAPTER 7

THE UNVEILING OF MYSELF

The sense of 'being myself' is an opening in the mind through which we may pass on our return home from the adventure of experience.

Imagine you are looking at a watercolour of a landscape under a cloudy sky and your attention is drawn to one of the clouds in the distance, which has caught the rays of the sun and is particularly bright.

Looking more closely at the painting, you notice that this is the only part of the paper where the artist hasn't applied any watercolour. From a distance the bare patch of white looks like an object *in* the painting, a cloud, one object amongst many, but from close up you see there's no paint there, only white paper.

The sense of 'being myself', or the knowledge 'I am', is the little patch of white paper in the painting of experience.

It seems to be an object *in* experience – one amongst many – but on coming closer we see that it is an opening, a portal, to our essential being or self, the ever-present background of all experience.

The paper is of course present not only in the little patch of sky but throughout the entire painting, just as our own being is present not only in the knowledge 'I am' but as the background of *all* experience. For this reason we say, '*I am* thinking', '*I am* walking', '*I am* breathing', '*I am* eating', and so on. Our being pervades all experience.

However, just as the paper is most visible when there is no watercolour covering it, so our essential being is most easily accessed at first through the simple feeling of 'being myself' or the knowledge 'I am'.

If we are fascinated by the content of the painting we will see only trees, fields, animals and sky, but as soon as our attention relaxes, we see the paper. We are in fact always seeing the paper but do not realise it, due to our exclusive focus on the content.

Likewise, when we are absorbed in the content of experience, we seem to lose touch with our being and are thus deprived of its innate peace and joy. Our being becomes so entangled in experience that it overlooks or forgets itself.

It no longer shines clearly as it is, open, unlimited, ever-present, inherently peaceful and unconditionally fulfilled, but is coloured and seemingly limited by our thoughts, feelings, sensations and perceptions. The knowledge 'I am' becomes 'I am tired', 'I am lonely', 'I am sad', and so on.

Experience eclipses being. All that is necessary is to allow being to outshine experience.

* * *

In a good watercolour the paint does not completely conceal the paper; it partially covers it with thin layers of wash, leaving the white paper to shine through even the darkest tones, imparting luminosity to the painting.

Likewise, no experience completely veils our essential self. Our experience lies like a watercolour wash on top of our self, which may as a result be partially obscured but is never completely eclipsed.

This is why the sense of 'being myself' remains present even in our darkest experiences. For instance, even when we feel 'I am depressed', the 'I am' is still shining there. As Albert

Camus said, 'In the depths of winter, I finally learned that within me there lay an invincible summer'.*

Just as the white paper gives coherence to the many different brushstrokes in the painting, so our being unifies the disparate elements of experience. If it were not for the unity of being pervading all experience, experience itself would be a chaos of fragmented thoughts, feelings, sensations and perceptions.

The unity of being shines in everyone's mind as the sense of 'being myself' or the knowledge 'I am', which is like a portal for one who is lost in experience, indicating the way back to our essential being and its innate peace.

*　　*　　*

Become aware of the experience of 'being myself' or the knowledge 'I am'.

The feeling of 'being myself', or the knowledge 'I am', seems to be an experience in the mind, whereas it is in fact an *absence* in the collage of objective experience. It is an opening to our essential, unlimited being, just as a hole in a piece of paper seems to be *in the paper* but is, in fact, an opening onto the vast space within which the paper is itself contained.

* From the essay 'Summer'.

The feeling of 'being myself', or the knowledge 'I am', gives us direct access to the reality of pure awareness *behind* and *prior to* the mind. It is the threshold of God's presence.

The suggestion that we become aware of the feeling of 'being myself', or the knowledge 'I am', implies that we are not already aware of our self but may *become* so. However, we are always aware of our self, just as the sun always illuminates itself. For this reason, *everyone* has a sense of 'being myself', although this knowledge is often diluted by objective experience.

It would be more accurate to suggest that we allow the feeling of 'being myself' or the knowledge 'I am' to bring us back to our self from the adventure of experience.

The pathless path from our self to our self is the essence of meditation and the heart of prayer. It is what Plotinus refers to as 'the flight of the alone to the alone'.*

* * *

We could say that there are two types of meditation: one in which we turn our attention *away* from the content

* From *The Enneads*, VI.9.II.

of experience and another in which we turn *towards* it.

The first is an inward-facing path which discriminates between our self and the objects of experience. It is a path of negation, exclusion and elimination: I am *not* this, *not* this. In theological terms, it is the Via Negativa; in the Zen tradition, the Great Death.

The second is an outward-facing path of openness, inclusion and allowing: I *am* this, *am* this. It is a path in which the apparent separation between our self and anyone or anything is dissolved. It is a path of unconditional love. It is the Via Positiva. It is the Great Rebirth in the Zen tradition.

Usually it is necessary to embark on the inward-facing path first, for most of us are so lost in the content of experience that we have almost completely overlooked or forgotten our own being.

Suffering is the price we pay for this forgetting. It is a call from our self to our self, saying, 'Turn around! Come back to me. I am what you are looking for, but you are looking for me in the wrong direction.'

This separation of our essential self from experience is the inward-facing path, in which our being is, in most cases gradually, occasionally suddenly, divested of the qualities it acquires from experience and stands revealed: silent, still, at peace.

This path is the means by which we recognise the inherently peaceful and unconditionally fulfilled nature of our being. It is the cure for suffering, the direct path to peace and happiness.

The outward-facing path is the means by which we recognise that our being is shared with everyone and everything. It is the remedy for conflict and the means by which kindness, harmony and justice are restored to humanity.

* * *

Experience itself is not inherently problematic. It is only when we abstract our self as a separate, independently existing entity or self that a situation becomes a problem. Openness turns into resistance.

When we allow our self to be defined by our thoughts, feelings, activities and relationships, we lose touch with our true nature and seem instead to become a temporary, finite self or ego, a separate person. Our suffering begins with that belief.

Having tried for most of our life to relieve our suffering through the acquisition of objects, substances, states of mind, activities and relationships, we eventually come to understand that the belief in being a separate person is the sole cause of that suffering.

As the Prodigal Son eventually turns to face his father, so we begin to question the person we seem to be: 'Who am I really? What do I mean when I say "I"?' Instead of being exclusively fascinated with the drama of our lives, we become profoundly interested in who we are.

It becomes clear that our suffering will not come to an end until this question is resolved. At some point the interest in the nature of 'I' eclipses all other interests. It is like falling in love with truth or reality.

As the self we seem to be is divested of the limitations that it appears to acquire from experience, our essential, irreducible nature is revealed. Experience no longer obscures our being; our being outshines experience.

Just as nothing happens to John Smith throughout the drama of *King Lear,* so nothing happens to our essential being. It did not previously become ignorant, nor does it now become enlightened.

To suggest that a person becomes enlightened is like suggesting that the sun rises in the morning. It is at best a concession to appearances but more often a misunderstanding.

The sun is always in the same place and shining with the same brightness. Likewise, our essential being never undergoes any change or evolution. It always shines with the same luminosity. It is simply concealed and revealed.

*   *   *

Just as John Smith freely adopts the character of King Lear in order to experience the roles of husband, father and king, so we freely assume the activities of thinking, feeling, sensing and perceiving in order to participate in the drama of experience. But just as John Smith never actually becomes King Lear, so we never become a separate self or person.

Having lost our self in experience and overlooked our innate peace and happiness, we embark on a search for them in the world, without realising that all we really long for is to be free of the limitations we have acquired from experience and to return to our true nature.

Nothing we acquire in life in terms of knowledge, objects, activities or relationships adds anything to our essential nature; nothing we lose takes anything away from it. It is only when we turn round to investigate the nature of our self that we find our way back to our inherent peace.

After a first glimpse of our true nature, the old habits of thinking and feeling will, in almost all cases, reappear and obscure it, so we will have to return to it again and again until, in time, we begin to be established in our being. We no longer visit it from time to time; we live there.

And just as John Smith eventually learns to play the role of King Lear without losing himself in it, so we are able to participate fully in experience without allowing it to veil our true nature and its innate joy.

To paraphrase Lao Tzu, 'Thus, one who knows their true nature never loses touch with its innate peace, however far they may travel and whatever they may do'.*

* Tao Te Ching, Chapter XXVI.

CHAPTER 8

THE JOY OF BEING

There is nothing extraordinary, complicated or difficult about recognising our essential nature and accessing its innate peace and happiness.

If our thoughts, feelings and perceptions are dense and heavy, then the light of being will seem to be dimmed by them. Our self will be 'endarkened' by experience. Enlightenment is simply the thinning of the layer of thoughts and feelings that veil being, just as clouds dissipate to reveal the ever-present sky.

Terms such as 'enlightenment', 'awakening' and 'liberation' have become so laden with association and misunderstanding that the truth to which they point is often overlooked. They tend to confer an extraordinary or exotic flavour on the simple recognition of our own being, implying it is a marvellous event that happens to a few special people, either spontaneously or as a result of strenuous discipline and practice.

Far from being extraordinary or exotic, our own being is the most ordinary, intimate and familiar experience. By comparison, the taste of tea, a feeling of sorrow or a thought about work tomorrow is exotic.

What may be extraordinary are the cultures to which many people have travelled, intellectually if not physically, in their quest for peace and happiness. People conflate the unusual traditions and customs of such cultures with the simple recognition of their own being and imagine, as a result, that it requires special practices, circumstances or relationships.

All these are distractions, albeit refined ones, from the simple knowing of our own being, from which one must sooner or later return. These cultures may hold the promise of the transcendent or mystical, appealing to our intuition that the fulfilment of our longing for peace and happiness is not to be found as an extension of our ordinary experience.

However, beneath our thoughts and feelings, and their expression in activities and relationships, we are all the same. If we had been able to take samples of the sense of 'being myself' from people at different periods in history and from different cultures, before their knowledge of their self was qualified by any particular experience, each sample would be identical. Being never changes.

Sooner or later we see with absolute clarity that the peace and happiness for which we long above all else can only be found within our own being and, as a result, we return to our self from the adventure of experience.

*   *   *

What is traditionally referred to as enlightenment is not an evolution or a development of our self. It is simply the revelation of the self that lies at the heart of all experience, irrespective of its content, the self we always and already are but have overlooked due to the clamour of experience.

The word 'revelation' comes from the Latin *revelare*, meaning 'to lay bare'. Enlightenment is simply the laying bare of our essential being – not how our being might become if we meditate for long enough or practise hard enough, or if we follow one teacher or tradition as opposed to another.

The recognition of our true nature as inherently peaceful and unconditionally fulfilled awareness is not something a person attains. Only awareness is aware.

It is awareness that loses itself in experience and seems to become a temporary, finite self or person, and then returns to or recognises itself again, just as John Smith veils himself with his own activity, seeming to become King Lear, and then unveils himself.

There is no such thing as an enlightened person. In the ultimate analysis, there simply is no independently existing person in the first place to be enlightened or not. Neither the Buddha nor Ramana Maharshi nor Meister Eckhart was enlightened.

There is only the light of the self, the light of our being, veiling itself with its own activity of thinking and perceiving, then unveiling and seeming to return to itself.

To be established in our true nature implies that experience has lost its capacity to veil its reality. As we sink more and more deeply into our being, the layers of experience which once seemed to obscure our true nature become progressively more transparent and, in time, shine with the light of being.

*   *   *

Our self is unconditioned, unqualified being. Know your self as that. Rest as that. Even the suggestion to rest as that is ultimately a concession to the separate self or ego, the one who believes they are other than that. It suggests we are a self who might or might not rest as that.

We *are* that, and its nature is already at rest! It would be more accurate, though again not completely so, simply to suggest, 'Be knowingly the inherently peaceful and unconditionally fulfilled presence that you always and already are'.

It is not necessary to change or get rid of any particular experience. We may be deeply depressed or madly in love; we may be walking down the street or drinking tea. Our self shines brightly in the midst of all experience, irrespective of its content.

All that is necessary is to allow our self to emerge from the background of experience, just as, when an image fades on a screen, the screen seems to emerge. Of course, the screen does not really emerge; it was fully visible all the time. It just seemed to be obscured by the image.

If our being seems to be obscured by experience and is, as a result, not clearly known, then all that is required is to soften the focus of our attention from its content and allow it to come back to our self. The self returns to itself and recognises or knows itself again.

*   *   *

We cannot become what we always and already are through any kind of practice, nor need we.

We can only become something that is *not* what we essentially are. We can *become* fifty years old. We can *become* tired. We can *become* married. We can *become* lonely. Our essential nature or self is prior to all becoming.

We may ignore, overlook or forget what we are, we may lose our self in experience, but even then we remain what we are, albeit unknowingly. Once we have allowed our being to be veiled by the content of experience, it will seem to be missing, and this apparent absence of our self will be accompanied by the loss of our innate peace and joy, the joy of simply being.

As a result of this lack, a great search is initiated which often takes us on a long journey around the world. But we are only searching for our being. Our self is travelling the world in search of itself!

If we look for the screen in an image, we will never find it, although all we are seeing is the screen. Likewise, if we look for our self in the content of experience, we will never find it, although all experience is pervaded by it. Our self does not seem to be missing because it is nowhere to be found; it seems to be missing because it is *everywhere*. It is hidden in plain view.

We do not have to go anywhere or do anything to find our self. In fact, anywhere we go or anything we do would seem to take us away from it, because going somewhere or doing something would reinforce the belief that our being is not present.

Having said that, for many people who feel their essential being and its innate peace and causeless joy are not present, the first stage may be to undertake some practice in order to access it. It is true that for a mind completely lost in objective experience, it may seem difficult to extricate itself and thus come back to itself.

In this case it may be necessary to engage in a preliminary practice, such as mantra meditation or focusing on the breath, in order to entice the mind away from its exclusive preoccupation with experience, before it is sufficiently free to return directly to its essence.

But such preliminary practices are rarely necessary, especially now that the simple, direct approach suggested here, divested of the local, temporal customs of the cultures in which it was previously expressed, is being made widely available.

The majority of people, whatever their race, religion or creed, and irrespective of the content of their experience, are capable of returning simply and directly from the adventure of experience to their self. That is the essence of meditation and the direct path to peace and happiness.

*   *   *

The unveiling of our essential self is sometimes accompanied by a relaxation of tension in the body and an expansion of the mind. These experiences may be pleasurable, but they are temporary side effects that may or may not occur. They may be extraordinary, but they have nothing to do with the recognition of our self or being.

There is nothing extraordinary about the recognition of our being, and it is quite possible that it will not be accompanied by any unusual signs, at least to begin with, in the body or mind.

In fact, the relaxation of the body and mind can happen so quietly and gradually that it is barely registered. In time, of course, the signs become evident and one who knows their own being exudes peace, clarity and warmth of heart.

It would be better not to look for any signs of enlightenment, but if we were to, the best we might find would be a causeless peace and joy that accompanies all experience, irrespective of its content. That would be the first sign in the mind of that which shines behind the mind.

This peace is not the result of what is or is not taking place in experience; it is the peace that underlies and pervades it. It is the 'peace that passeth understanding'.

CHAPTER 9

THE WORLD AND MYSELF ARE ONE

I n the first stage of meditation, the inward-facing path or the way of discrimination, we extricate our essential self from everything we are aware of. Awareness turns away from the objects of experience and recognises itself as the subject of experience, the knower of the known.

I am aware of thoughts, feelings, sensations and perceptions, but am not myself any such object. I am that which knows or is aware of them. I am the knowing element in all experience.

In the second stage of meditation, the outward-facing path or the way of inclusion, we face the objective content of experience from which we previously turned away, but we no longer lose our self in it. We allow it to merge into our self. We do not go towards experience; we let it come to us.

Experience always takes place in the same place: the place-less place where awareness is, where I am.

We cannot even say that experience comes to us, as if it came from a distance. No experience is at a distance from our self or other than our self. It is our self – knowing, being aware or awareness itself – that assumes all forms of experience. Experience is the *activity* of awareness.

All there is to experience is the knowing of it. All experience of thinking, sensing and perceiving is a colouring of awareness, a modulation of what I am.

Once this is clear, it is no longer necessary to take the inward-facing path. Indeed, it is no longer necessary to take any path. There is no pathway from our self to our self.

From time to time, we may still turn away from the content of experience to rest in being, *as* being, but we no longer do so because objective experience is problematic.

Experience has lost its capacity to veil our self from our self. It has lost its ability to disguise its reality and instead shines with it. We are equally at home in the presence and the absence of experience.

We are equally at peace resting in our own being as we are in the midst of activities and relationships. The conflict between awareness and its objects has dissolved. The distinction between life and meditation has come to an end.

* * *

The word 'existence' comes from two Latin words, *ex*, 'out of' or 'from', and *sistere*, 'to stand', indicating that something that exists 'stands out from' its background, just as an object in a movie seems to stand out from the screen.

What is the background from which everything that exists stands out? Being!

Nothing in a movie is distinct from the screen or has its own independent reality. Nor, in real life, does any person or object *exist* in its own right; they are names and forms of a single, infinite and indivisible being.

Everything in a movie is a colouring of the screen. Existence is a movement of being.

The being or presence shared by all people and things is infinite, and everything that is seen, heard, touched, tasted or smelt is its transitory name and form.

Everything we encounter is a manifestation of that which truly is: pure being, or, in religious language, God's presence.

No object exists independently of God's being. This is what is meant by the Islamic prayer *La ilaha illallah*, or 'There is no God but God'. No thing has its own independent existence. No person or object is an entity unto itself. Nothing actually exists!

If properly understood, this is not a nihilistic statement. On the contrary, it is an affirmation of the fact that every object or event we encounter is a temporary name and form of eternal, infinite being. As the Sufis say, 'Wherever you look, there is the face of God'.

The apparent existence of things is borrowed from that which truly *is*, God's infinite being, just as the apparent reality of objects in a movie is borrowed from the reality, relatively speaking, of the screen.

Things don't have their own existence; being has things. Selves don't have awareness; awareness has selves.

We do not think of things because they exist; they seem to exist because we think of them. Thought abstracts discrete objects and selves from the reality of God's infinite and indivisible being.

To feel this reality in the midst of experience is to know beauty and love. It is God's presence shining in and as existence.

* * *

If we make an investigation into our self, we find only un-limited, self-aware being, 'I am'. If we go outwards towards the objects of the world, we find only infinite being. How many infinite beings can there be?

The great recognition at the heart of all the religious and spiritual traditions is that the am-ness of our self and the is-ness of things is the same infinite and indivisible whole or reality, made of pure awareness or spirit.

This reality, shining on the inside as the knowledge 'I am' and on the outside as the knowledge 'It is', is modulated by thought and perception and appears as a multiplicity and diversity of objects and selves, just as everything that appears in a dream at night is the activity of a single, indi-visible mind.

Awareness is the essence of our self; being is the essence of the world. These are not two. Their unity is refracted by thought and perception, but never actually ceases to be the same infinite, indivisible reality or whole.

The revelation of this reality is the impulse behind all great art. It was for this reason that the filmmaker Pier Paolo Pasolini said, 'I want my films to restore to reality its original sacred significance'. It is what Cézanne meant when he said of his painting, 'I want my work to give people a taste of nature's eternity'. And it is what Bach was referring to in religious language when he said, 'All my work is composed for the glory of God'.

The is-ness of all things and the am-ness of all selves is the same infinite, indivisible, self-aware being, known in religion as the presence of God, in science as consciousness, often referred to as awareness and commonly known as 'I'.

CHAPTER 10

PEACE AND HAPPINESS LIE IN THE DEPTHS
OF OUR BEING

Once infinite being has contracted into the form of a person, it loses touch with its innate peace and happiness. For this reason, suffering and the search for happiness inevitably accompany the forgetting of our self.

This search can never be satisfied by the acquisition of an object, substance, activity, state of mind or relationship. Peace and happiness are the very nature of our self when it is no longer limited by experience. Relieved of limitation, our true nature simply shines by itself.

The feeling of 'being myself', or the knowledge 'I am', is a treasure that we all carry around with us without realising it. It is our true wealth. We are like one who shops for coloured stones in the market without knowing they have a diamond in their pocket.

The peace and happiness for which we all long reside in the simple knowing of our self, in the knowledge 'I am', in the awareness of being.

Suffering ensues when we allow awareness of objects to eclipse awareness of being. Happiness is revealed when we allow awareness of being to outshine awareness of objects.

*　　*　　*

It may seem legitimate to object that happiness, like all other feelings, comes and goes. However, in reality happiness is like a patch of blue sky appearing among the clouds on an overcast day.

At first glance the blue sky looks like a temporary appearance *within* the clouds, just as happiness seems at first to be a fleeting experience arising *between* our afflictive emotions. The blue sky is, of course, the continuous background of the passing clouds, just as happiness is the ever-present background of all changing feelings.

And just as the sky is never agitated by the weather, so the background of awareness is never disturbed by experience. Its nature is peace.

The clouds add nothing to the sky, just as experience adds nothing to our true nature of awareness. Our true nature is complete in itself. It needs nothing from experience and is thus happiness itself.

This does not invalidate experience or imply we should not attend to it. It simply suggests that it is a mistake to invest our happiness in it.

The sky never changes, although it is the very stuff from which the clouds are made, just as awareness is not modified, enhanced or diminished by experience, although it is the substance of experience itself.

All the great religious and spiritual traditions recognise that awareness of being, shining in each of us as the experience of 'being myself' or the knowledge 'I am', *is* happiness itself.

The peace and happiness for which we long above all else, and habitually seek outside ourself, reside in the simple knowing of our own being as it is.

* * *

Just as empty space, before anything appears in it, cannot be agitated, for there is nothing there which could do so, our essential self or being, before the arising of any experience, contains nothing in itself, other than itself, which could possibly disturb it.

And just as the condition of empty space does not change when objects appear within it, so the nature of our essential self remains the same during any experience, irrespective of its content. Thus, its natural condition is peace. It does not need to be *made* peaceful by effort, practice or discipline; it simply needs to be recognised as such. It recognises itself.

The 'peace that passeth understanding' is inherent in our own being – it *is* our own being – and is not derived from objective experience. It is only when we allow our self to be coloured by the content of experience that we appear to assume its qualities. If our thoughts, sensations or perceptions are agitated, we seem to acquire their agitation. We lose our self in experience and our innate peace is temporarily obscured.

However, just as the screen upon which a movie plays is never itself fragmented by the appearance of objects and characters, so our essential self or being is never divided, modified or harmed by experience. It is always in the same pristine condition, lacking nothing, holding on to nothing, seeking nothing. Its nature is ease, fulfilment, peace.

Happiness is the very nature of our self. It is our self's knowledge of itself. The knowing of being is itself happiness.

Happiness is unconditional because it is not caused by or dependent upon anything that does or does not take place in experience. When Krishnamurti said, 'I don't mind what happens', he didn't mean to imply that he did not care. He simply meant that his happiness was not invested in the content of experience.

* * *

If happiness is the nature of our self and, like our self, remains present throughout all experience, we might wonder why we do not feel at peace and happy all the time.

The answer is simply that our innate happiness is obscured, at least partially, when we allow our self to become lost in the content of experience and, as a result, we cease knowing our self as we essentially are. The forgetting of our true nature eclipses our innate happiness, and suffering follows.

We may not feel at peace and happy all the time, but even in our darkest moments the longing for happiness remains. This longing is our true nature shining in the midst of suffering. It is our self calling itself back to itself. There is either happiness or the longing for happiness, but never its absence.

However, happiness cannot be known objectively. In order to objectify an experience and name it, we must first stand apart from it and know it at a distance. Just as one cannot take a step away from oneself, so we cannot separate our self from our self and know its innate happiness as an objective experience. By contrast, unhappiness is a mixture of thoughts and feelings. It is always known objectively.

We cannot know happiness; we can only be it. We cannot be unhappy; we can only know it.

* * *

Instead of being aware of thoughts, images, feelings, sensations and perceptions, we may simply be aware of our self. We rest in the feeling of being or the knowledge 'I am'.

In this self-resting, the ordinary, intimate, familiar self that we always and already are, but often overlook, is simply revealed.

This unlimited, ever-present, imperturbable and inherently fulfilled being that we essentially are cannot be attained by effort, practice or discipline. It loses itself in its own activity and then returns to itself. It overlooks itself and then remembers itself. It is concealed and then revealed.

We do not have to go anywhere or do anything in order to be in touch with the peace and the happiness that are the nature of our self. We simply notice that we *are* that.

It is for this reason that the sage Ashtavakra said, 'Happiness belongs to that supremely lazy person for whom even blinking is too much trouble'.*

---

* Ashtavakra Gita, Chapter XVI, Verse IV.

CHAPTER II

ESTABLISHMENT IN OUR TRUE NATURE

Everything we have ever truly longed for is to be found in the simple knowing of our own being as it essentially is.

At first, most of us glimpse our essential being in the background of experience, only to find it, through force of habit, almost immediately eclipsed by the content of experience. In this case, we may repeatedly trace our way back to our self until we begin to be established in it, *as* it.

It is like meeting a stranger at a lecture or party. Initially we catch sight of them briefly and, although we have never seen them before, our interest is awakened. We seem to recognise them. For some time their memory disturbs us, as if calling us to something we have always known but forgotten.

Two weeks later we come across them again in the super-market. It seems a coincidence, but at the same time we are not surprised. We arrange to meet for coffee and begin to become acquainted, and notice that the deeper the acquaintance, the greater the desire to know more. Next we meet for dinner and soon we spend a weekend together. Some months later we move in and, hopefully, live happily ever after!

For most of us, the recognition of our true nature takes place in a similar way: repeated glimpses followed by gradual establishment, although in rare cases the first recognition is sufficient and is never again eclipsed by experience. Either way, once we have had that first glimpse, our life is never the same again. We have been disturbed by something that is recognised to be at once new and familiar.

After this first recognition, we become curious. We may seek out a friend, read a book, watch a video or simply investigate within our self. Sooner or later we are led back to the same experience, to our own being in its original, naked condition before it is qualified by experience, and again we taste its innate peace and joy. We rest there, for how long we do not know, since this does not take place in the same time as our everyday experience.

Eventually, through force of habit, objective experience draws us away from our self. However, we notice that each time we 'return' to our self, we seem to rest there a little longer, and as we do so, the habit of getting lost in experience is gradually eroded.

For some time it may still seem that we go back and forth between our objective experience and the peace of our essential being, but eventually we develop the ability not only to return to our self in the background of experience but to remain there in the midst of experience.

Experience has lost its power to take us away from our self and to veil our innate peace and happiness. We no longer lose our self in the content of experience. We are becoming established in our true nature. We have come home.

*   *   *

When our self or being sheds the qualities it inherits from experience, it loses its agitation and its essential nature of peace is revealed. It loses its sense of lack and its innate joy is exposed.

The identification of our self with the content of experience creates the separate self or ego around which most of our lives revolve. Divested of the limitations inherent in experience, our original freedom is restored. Our self is released from its existential sense of lack and fear of death.

Occasionally this recognition is so full and complete that the old habits of thinking and feeling on behalf of a temporary, finite self, and the agitation and unhappiness that accompany them, never reappear. However, in almost all cases these habits come back and continue to be expressed in our activities and relationships.

Although the belief that we are a temporary, finite, separate self has been uprooted through understanding, old habits have a momentum which may still cause them to arise, like a boat on the ocean whose engines are turned off but that carries on moving for some time. In this case it will be necessary to trace our way back to our self again and again until we are stabilised there.

Each time we return to our self, the pathway gets shorter and easier, and experience increasingly loses its capacity to take us away. Gradually, we become established in and as our true nature.

As this happens, peace and happiness begin to pervade our experience from the inside. They not only permeate our thoughts and feelings but begin to express themselves in our activities and relationships.

In time, the body and mind are transformed from the inside by this recognition, so there is a change, although it may not be dramatic. In fact, the mind may not at first realise what is happening and only gradually come to know that it is being transformed.

Slowly, all realms of experience are colonised by the peace of our true nature and it begins to communicate itself effortlessly, with or without words, in all of our interactions.

At first we have a glimpse or a taste of our true nature, then we establish ourself in it, and then we lead a life, to the best of our ability, in a way that is consistent with and an expression of its intrinsic qualities.

* * *

At every moment, and in all situations, we are free to allow experience to veil our innate peace or to remain transparent to it. Our experience will appear in accordance with whichever possibility we choose. If we allow it to veil being, then it will conform to that possibility. If we remain in touch with being, our experience will be increasingly permeated by its innate peace.

Once it becomes clear that our being remains untouched by all experience, irrespective of its content, the activities of seeking and resisting that characterise the apparently separate self or ego begin to subside.

We may continue to seek refuge on a daily basis in the privacy and silence of our own being, but we do not feel that we leave that refuge when we go out into the world of experience. We take our self with us wherever we go. We are safe, not only in the sanctuary of the heart but in the midst of all experience.

This does not mean that we no longer feel grief or sorrow; it simply means that we no longer feel the need to defend against them. We are totally open to them, indeed to all experience, and as a result they lose their afflictive quality.

Nor is it necessary to seek or resist any particular experience for the purpose of finding peace or happiness, for all experience begins to shine equally with it. A feeling of sameness pervades everything.

This does not mean that we no longer appreciate the qualities of particular experiences, but our view becomes even. Experience no longer holds the promise of happiness or the threat of unhappiness.

A mind that is accustomed to resting frequently in its essence becomes increasingly saturated with peace. When such a mind returns to experience, it does not leave that peace behind. It takes it with itself, and its activities of thinking, feeling, sensing, perceiving, acting and relating become an expression, a communication and a celebration of that peace.

W. B. Yeats describes this in his poem 'Vacillation': 'It seemed, so great my happiness, that I was blessèd and could bless'.*

To be blessed is to be in touch with the peace and joy of our true nature. In religious language, it is to feel God's presence in one's heart.

To the extent that each of us is in touch with this presence, so it communicates itself, with or without words, shedding its light on everyone and everything with whom we come in contact.

* Verse IV.

CHAPTER 12

KEEP THE NAME 'I' SACRED

I is the name that whatever knows or is aware of itself gives to itself. A rock does not know itself; a flower does not know itself; nor does a tree, a cat, a dog or a person. Only awareness is aware, therefore only awareness knows or is aware of itself.

The name 'I' is not the name that a person gives to their self; it is the name that *awareness* gives to itself and should be reserved for awareness alone.

In awareness's knowledge of itself there are no limits. Its knowledge of itself is infinite. The name 'I' should always refer to this infinite, self-aware being. It is the name of God.

God's presence shines in each of us as the ordinary, intimate and familiar experience of 'being myself' or 'I am'.

Our knowledge of our self is awareness's knowledge of itself, which is God's knowledge of Himself.

*   *   *

Be aware of the experience of 'being myself'.

Before we know anything else, we know that we *are*. We know our own being. We know that I am. The knowledge 'I am', the awareness of being, is the mind's primary knowledge.

This knowledge is the same for everyone. The awareness of being in Hitler was identical to the awareness of being in Ramana Maharshi or the Buddha. Their thoughts, feelings, activities and relationships were different, but their essential self was the same. In one case it was obscured by experience and in the others it was not.

Nor is the recognition of our own being extraordinary or difficult. Everybody has the sense of 'being myself' or the experience 'I am'. If we were to ask any of the seven billion people on earth, 'Are you present?' or 'Are you aware?', as long as they understood the question, they would answer, 'Yes, I am'.

Everyone knows their own being; that is, the being in everyone knows itself. The expression 'I am', before anything has been attached to it, is the simplest expression of self-knowledge, for in order to say 'I am', I must *know* that I am.

Ramana Maharshi once said that God's statement to Moses, 'I am that I am', is the highest formulation of truth in any spiritual tradition. That is why the name 'I' in this approach is considered to be sacred. It is the holy name, the name of God.

All that is necessary is to sound the name 'I' or 'I am' once in our mind and allow our self to be drawn into its referent. It is for this reason that the Zen master Ikkyu said, 'Of all the koans, "I" is the highest'.*

* * *

All experience is a temporary colouring of unconditioned, unlimited, self-aware being. Experience is the activity of being; being is experience at rest.

Every experience is eternal, infinite being, God's being, clothing itself in its own activity, appearing to itself, through the lens of perception, as the world. Divested of its clothing, of its limitations, it is revealed as joy. This is what William Blake was describing when he said,

* From *Crow with No Mouth*.

'Every bird that cuts the airy way is an immense world of delight enclosed by the five senses'.*

Do not allow experience to persuade you that you are anything other than ever-present, inherently peaceful, unconditionally fulfilled being, the being you share with everything and everyone.

Allow your self to be coloured by experience temporarily, but do not become limited by it. To say and identify with the statements 'I am sad', 'I am lonely', 'I am tired', 'I am hungry', 'I am a man' or 'I am a woman' is to allow infinite being to become limited and personal.

When 'I am' becomes 'I am this or that', it seems to cease being infinite and become finite. The separate self or ego is an apparent and ultimately illusory limitation self-assumed by infinite being.

The finite cannot exist alongside the infinite, for if the finite displaced a part of the infinite, the infinite would no longer be infinite. There is no room in the infinite for the finite. Thus, to believe 'I am a man, a woman or a person' is to impose a limit on God's infinite being. It is to

* From *The Marriage of Heaven and Hell*.

deny the existence of God's infinite being, and that is blasphemy.

It is not blasphemous to say, 'I am God', although it is not appropriate to do so. What is blasphemous is to believe and feel 'I am a being apart from God's being. I am a self unto myself, a temporary, finite self, separate from all others and from God.'

That is the original sin, the root cause of all other so-called sins. It is the departure from the Garden of Eden. In the Vedantic tradition it is called ignorance, meaning not stupidity but rather the ignoring of the true and only self, ever-present, unlimited awareness, or God's infinite, self-aware being.

To say and believe 'I am sick' or 'I lack something' is to identify oneself as finite. Only something that is finite can lack something or be in a state of disease. That which truly is, the 'I' of each of us, knows no lack or disease.

Whenever we feel sad, lonely, anxious or depressed, we should pause and notice that the feeling is not essential to the knowledge 'I am'.

Return to the 'I am'. Keep the 'I' sacred. Do not allow your self to be tarnished by association with anything other than your self. Do not give your self away to experience.

*   *   *

This 'I', our essential, irreducible self, is universal, unlimited and impersonal, and is thus referred to as God.

This mixture of God's infinite, self-aware being and the qualities of experience produces the illusion of a temporary, finite, individual self or ego. But the self of the apparently individual self *is* God's self, the only self there is. The 'I' in each of us is God's presence, the only presence there is.

The personal self is not *one* kind of self and God's infinite being *another* kind of self. The personal self is simply God's infinite being mixed with the limitations of experience. There are not two selves, one higher and the other lower, one personal and one impersonal.

There is one self, if we can call it that, one infinite, self-aware being, freely assuming the form of each of our minds, thereby seeming to limit itself and become separate, but never in fact ceasing to be itself alone.

The personal self or ego is simply a self-assumed and imaginary limitation of the true and only self of infinite being. And just as there is no distance from King Lear to John

Smith, so there is no distance from the self that we seem to be to the self that we essentially are.

Therefore, there is no room for a practice, a practitioner, a path or an effort. Any effort would be an apparent movement away from our self, towards something other than our self. We cannot go to our self by discipline or effort; we go there by love and surrender. The pathway from our self to our self *is* our self.

In the words of the Sufi mystic Balyani, 'He sent Himself from Himself, through Himself to Himself. There is no means or intermediary other than Him. There is no difference between the sender, that which is sent and the one to whom it is sent.'*

* * *

The knowledge 'I am' or the feeling of 'being myself' is a hint or trace of God's presence. It gives the mind the direction in which to go if it wants to know its own essence and reality. It is the direct path to peace and happiness.

All we need do is to stay with the sense of 'being myself' or take the thought 'I am' and allow it to lead us to its source,

---

* Awhad al-din Balyani, *Know Yourself*, translated by Cecilia Twinch (Beshara Publications, 2011).

our being, God's being, before it is qualified or conditioned by experience.

To abide in the 'I am' is the highest meditation. It is the essence of the way of knowledge, the investigation into the nature of the self. It takes the mind directly to its essence.

It is also the most sacred prayer. It is the essence of the way of love or devotion. It takes us directly to God's presence in the heart. It is the prayer for which all other prayers are a preparation.

In resting in our own being, the paths of knowledge and devotion are united.

CHAPTER 13

THE DIVINE NAME

The knowledge 'I am' or the feeling of 'being myself' is a hint of the Beloved. It is the perfume of God's presence in the heart. To give oneself entirely to the 'I am' is to lose oneself in God's presence. This loss of one's apparent self in God's presence is the ultimate surrender.

As the Sufi mystic Bayazid Bastami said, 'Forgetfulness of self is remembrance of God'.*

Prior to creation, God must be and God must know. More accurately, God signifies the knowing of being, prior to form. In fact, prior to creation there is no 'prior'.

The common name for the knowing of being is 'I', for 'I' is the name that whatever knows itself gives to itself.

---

* Quoted in James Fadiman and Robert Frager, *Essential Sufism* (HarperCollins, 1997).

If God were to give Himself a name He would call Himself 'I'.

Thus, the name 'I' is the first form of God. It is the divine name. It is the name of the nameless. It is the first utterance as infinite being emerges from the formless into form.

'I' is the Logos or Word which, before it is uttered, is God's unmanifest intelligence. Once named, it is the portal through which manifestation is ushered.

Krishnamurti referred to this as 'the first and last freedom'. It is the portal through which the separate self reclaims its freedom from the tyranny of experience, and the same portal through which infinite being travels in the opposite direction as it passes out of eternity into time, forgoing its freedom in favour of experience.

As Jesus says, 'I am the door. If anyone enters by Me, he will be saved.'* The name 'I' is the doorway through which the finite mind passes as it is divested of the limitations it acquires from experience and is returned to its natural condition of peace and joy.

* Gospel of John, 10:9.

'I' is the divine name, and each of us calls our self 'I'. God has given us His name to remind us that our self is His self: infinite, intimate, impersonal being, the only self there is, the self of all selves, the being in all existence.

Know that each of our individual names is one of the many names of God's infinite being. That is why it is called a Christian name; it is the name of Christ in us.

When we hear our name called, we say, 'Yes! I am here!' In that moment, the sound of our name draws our attention to pure being, to the experience 'I am', before it is coloured by experience. God's presence shines briefly in us, before it acquires an attribute and seems to become a person.

* * *

Do not allow the name 'I' to become personalised by thoughts, feelings, sensations and perceptions. Do not allow it to be tarnished by experience. Become accustomed to taking refuge from your thoughts, feelings, sensations and perceptions and simply resting in being, as being.

We cannot really rest *in* being, because we already *are* being, so rest knowingly *as* your essential being, independent of whatever experience may be present.

Our own being is closer to us than our breath, closer to us than our most intimate thoughts and feelings. In fact, it is not close to us. It *is* us.

We cannot find it; we can only be it knowingly. We cannot lose it; we can only overlook it. Rest as that. Do not take refuge in a teaching, a situation or a relationship. Take refuge in your self.

If we are unhappy or feel any sense of lack, instead of seeking to fulfil our longing, we should seek the *source* of our longing. The source of our longing is 'I', 'myself', the one who is unhappy.

If we go deeply into that sense of 'I', we will, either gradually or suddenly, be divested of the limitations we have acquired from experience, and that for which we were in search will be revealed as our very own self.

The 'I' that longs is a colouring of the 'I' that is longed for. Divested of this colouring, it is revealed as the true and only 'I' of infinite awareness, God's presence. As Ramana Maharshi said, 'When the "I" is divested of the "I", only "I" remains'.

* * *

When I was at boarding school in England, we used to sing a hymn in chapel every Sunday evening:

> God be in my head and in my understanding;
> God be in my eyes and in my looking;
> God be in my mouth and in my speaking;
> God be in my heart and in my thinking;
> God be at my end and at my departing.

As much as I loved the hymn, little did I realise at the time that the self in myself *is* God's being. The simple feeling of being, or the knowledge 'I am', *is* God's presence in us, as us.

Do not allow 'I' to become personal or finite. If a thought or feeling arises on behalf of a personal self, or an activity or relationship is initiated in its service, pause and investigate. Hold up the mirror of understanding. The personal self cannot stand the bright light of awareness. Allow it to come to an end in understanding.

In this way, our lives cease serving and perpetuating the fears, desires and anxieties that characterise the separate self or ego and begin to express, share and celebrate the qualities of peace, love, joy, justice and compassion that are innate in our essential nature.

* * *

The knowledge 'I am' is infinite consciousness shining in each of our finite minds. The feeling of 'being myself' is God's presence pervading our hearts. 'I' is the divine name in each of us.

Every time we think or say 'I', we may follow it, like Ariadne's golden thread, to the luminous being that not only lies behind all experience, although it is often found there first, but shines in the midst of all experience, and *is* all experience.

In the knowledge 'I' or the simple experience of 'being myself', the peace and happiness for which we long above all else can be found quietly shining.

To feel that our essential being is shared with all others is love. It is the means by which conflicts between individuals, communities and nations may be resolved.

The recognition that we share our being with all things places us in harmony with nature, and will thereby restore humanity's relationship with the planet.

The knowledge of being must, as such, be the foundation of any truly civilised society. All that is necessary is to go to the feeling of 'being myself' or the thought 'I am' and sink deeply into it.

All that we truly long for lives there, in the depths of our being. If we turn towards it, it will take us into itself.

THE ESSENCE OF MEDITATION SERIES

The Essence of Meditation Series presents meditations
on the essential, non-dual understanding that lies
at the heart of all the great religious and spiritual traditions,
compiled from contemplations led by Rupert Spira
at his meetings and retreats. This simple, contemplative
approach, which encourages a clear seeing of one's
experience rather than any kind of effort or discipline,
leads the reader to an experiential understanding of their
own essential being and the peace and fulfilment that are
inherent within it.

Being Aware of Being Aware
The Essence of Meditation Series, Volume I
Sahaja Publications & New Harbinger Publications 2017

Being Myself
The Essence of Meditation Series, Volume II
Sahaja Publications & New Harbinger Publications 2021

PUBLICATIONS BY RUPERT SPIRA

The Transparency of Things – Contemplating the Nature of Experience

Non-Duality Press 2008, Sahaja Publications & New Harbinger Publications 2016

Presence, Volume I – The Art of Peace and Happiness

Non-Duality Press 2011, Sahaja Publications & New Harbinger Publications 2016

Presence, Volume II – The Intimacy of All Experience

Non-Duality Press 2011, Sahaja Publications & New Harbinger Publications 2016

The Ashes of Love – Sayings on the Essence of Non-Duality

Non-Duality Press 2013, Sahaja Publications 2016

*The Light of Pure Knowing – Thirty Meditations
on the Essence of Non-Duality*

Sahaja Publications 2014

*Transparent Body, Luminous World – The Tantric Yoga
of Sensation and Perception*

Sahaja Publications 2016

The Nature of Consciousness – Essays on the Unity of Mind and Matter

Sahaja Publications & New Harbinger Publications 2017

A Meditation on I Am

Sahaja Publications & New Harbinger Publications 2021

www.rupertspira.com